Raintree is an imprint of Capstone Global Library Limited, a company incorporated in England and Wales having its registered office at 264 Banbury Road, Oxford, OX2 7DY – Registered company number: 6695582

www.raintree.co.uk
myorders@raintree.co.uk

Edited by Michelle Bisson
Designed by Russell Griesmer
Original illustrations © Capstone Global Library Limited 2019
Picture research by Morgan Walters
Production by Tori Abraham
Originated by Capstone Global Library Ltd
Printed and bound in India

ISBN 978 1 4747 6022 5
22 21 20 19 18
10 9 8 7 6 5 4 3 2 1

British Library Cataloguing in Publication Data
A full catalogue record for this book is available from the British Library.

Acknowledgements
We would like to thank the following for permission to reproduce photographs: Alamy: PPJF Military Collection, 27; ASSOCIATED PRESS: Axel Heimken, 11; Getty Images: Kevin Mazur, 6, Mark Boster, 16; iStockphoto: damedeeso, 7, gmutlu, 14; Shutterstock: Alisara Zilch, cover, design element throughout, balabolka, cover, design element throughout, catwalker, 15, chanpipat, 25, charles taylor, 21, Eladora, (head) cover, karen roach, 29, MacrovectorBottom of Form, nopporn, 20, notkoo, 5, o Samsara o, 24, panuwat phimpha, 18, Rawpixel.com, 26, SpeedKingz, 28, topform, cover, design element throughout; Wikimedia: Jscott, 8, Laurens van Lieshout, 13

Every effort has been made to contact copyright holders of material reproduced in this book. Any omissions will be rectified in subsequent printings if notice is given to the publisher.

CONTENTS

CHAPTER 1

WHAT IS MEDIA LITERACY?

Think about it. You have the whole world in one device. Or quite a lot of it, anyway. Everyone who has a smartphone, tablet or computer can connect to the internet. They can share photos and post opinions. They can send a string of texts or emails. They can stay in close touch with their whole social circle.

The wider world is easy to get to as well. All it takes is a few keystrokes, voice commands or clicks. People can find global news, entertainment and just about any information they need. We're all citizens of the digital world. That means media literacy is more important than ever. But what does media literacy mean?

DID YOU KNOW?

Media has three main purposes – to persuade, to entertain and to inform. An important part of media literacy is understanding which is which. Media literacy is the ability to gather information from all media sources and **analyse** it intelligently.

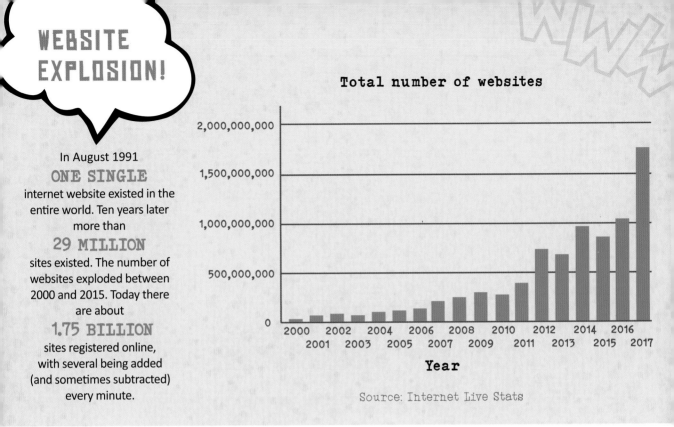

In August 1991
ONE SINGLE
internet website existed in the entire world. Ten years later more than
29 MILLION
sites existed. The number of websites exploded between 2000 and 2015. Today there are about
1.75 BILLION
sites registered online, with several being added (and sometimes subtracted) every minute.

Total number of websites

Source: Internet Live Stats

We get information from various forms of media, including newspapers, magazines, radio and TV. We also view billboards, flyers and posters. And don't forget the internet, with its 1.75 billion or so websites worldwide. And that doesn't include the millions of separate social media accounts on sites such as Snapchat, Instagram, Facebook and Twitter. That's a lot of media.

⭐ **analyse** examine something carefully in order to understand it

⭐ **social media** websites and software applications that allow users to connect through the internet

Being bombarded by media has become a part of modern life. So how does a person make sense of the information overload and sort through it wisely? How do you find the information you need while avoiding what is useless, distracting and simply untrue? How do you make sure you're not fooled by ads that look like news stories?

The answer is media literacy. It is a skill that helps people weed out false information and tall tales. And stops them being caught in a faker's web.

Media literacy also allows you to focus on what is useful. For example, think of all the pets that are separated from their families during natural disasters or other troubles. In the **predigital** age not much could be done to help. But

People have found their lost pets after posting about them on social media.

now internet users turn to social media to **reunite** lost animals with their owners. It has resulted in many heartwarming success stories. Who wouldn't want to be part of – or even start – such a positive project now that it's possible? Understanding how to use media can help.

⭐ **predigital** before the time of computer technology

⭐ **reunite** bring together again

CHAPTER 2

THE ROOTS OF INTERNET CONNECTION

In January 1978, Chicago, USA, was hit by one of the city's worst snowstorms. Nobody could get around. But the Great Blizzard of 1978 gave two young computer programmers a chance to go down in history. While the storm raged, Ward Christensen and Randy Suess began work on something that would change the world.

Ward Christensen with the first BBS

It was a software program called CBBS, the computer bulletin board system. It was later shortened to BBS. It was a groundbreaking moment. At that time the internet was very small and few people had computers. But some people who did could now connect to Christensen's BBS. To do so they used their landline telephones and a dial-up modem. Users posted news and announcements, as they might have done on a bulletin board hanging on a wall. They could send each other messages.

The whole system was very slow. But its value came in connecting a large group of people in more than one geographical area. Pretty soon BBS networks were cropping up in one city after another.

By the early 1990s more and more people had logged onto the networks. They were excited by the possibilities of being connected through cyberspace. The roots of social media had sprouted.

 modem piece of electronic equipment that sends information between computers by telephone lines

 cyberspace online world of computer networks

The first message board lit a great spark. But the slow and clunky BBS model was doomed. By the mid-1990s people were discovering new and better ways to connect with one another on their computers. One of the first ways was email, which quickly gained popularity. Email was great for both personal and business uses.

America Online (AOL) was one of the first and most successful companies to offer email service to people for a fee. AOL took online communication another giant leap forward in 1997. It offered users AIM – America Online Instant Messaging. Now people could chat with friends in real time, on their computer screens. While they talked, they could do other things as well. They could even swap IMs with more than one person at a time.

DID YOU KNOW?

One of the very first instant messaging systems for kids was created in 1983. Its creator was Mark Jenks, a teenager from Wisconsin, USA. It was called "Talk". When pupils at his school logged on, they could send each other private messages.

This AOL icon became well known
around the world.

Other companies soon tried to follow AOL's lead. But in the late 1990s and early 2000s AOL dominated. Sometimes as many as 18 million users were sending and receiving instant messages at the same time. But then communication methods changed and AOL lost its grip on the big numbers.

Instant messaging wasn't the only tool being developed. Companies began to create social media and gaming sites of all types. Everyone wanted to outdo AOL and AIM. The competitors added fun features and their own messaging systems. The sites began to draw many users.

A new internet sensation launched in May 1997, at exactly the same time AIM appeared. Called Six Degrees, it offered instant messaging. It also gave users the power to create personal profiles and friends lists. They could even search each other's friends lists. Today that's no big deal. But in the 1990s, it was unheard of. Word spread quickly and users flocked to Six Degrees. At its peak the site had more than 1 million registered members.

Six Degrees lasted only a few years. Still, its early success pushed other companies to build their own social networking sites. As one rose, others fell. The social media war was on.

Six degrees of separation

Six Degrees got its name from the idea that only six degrees of separation exist between any two people on Earth. In other words, you and five of your acquaintances connect to everyone – including any celebrity. Research proves the point – almost! In 2006, Microsoft studied the records of 30 billion electronic conversations among 180 million people in various countries. It was about half the world's instant messaging traffic at the time. They found that it took about 6.6 hops to connect any two pairs of people messaging online.

There's even a game based on the idea, called Six Degrees of Kevin Bacon. Players try to find links between Hollywood actor Kevin Bacon and any other actor, dead or alive. The idea is that it shouldn't take more than six steps of connection.

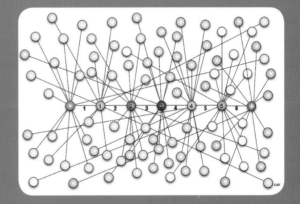

CHAPTER 3

THE SOCIAL MEDIA EXPLOSION

A social networking site called Friendster took the lead in the social media war in 2002. But its popularity didn't last. Only a year later, the young social media crowd turned to MySpace. Two former Friendster members created it.

MySpace had many great familiar features and new ones as well. Users could create a custom-designed profile page of their own. Then they could add music, videos and a page featuring pictures of their "top friends". All this attracted millions of registered members worldwide.

Friendster was a pioneer in social media.

But the real monster among social media options would soon take over the field. That monster, called The Facebook, launched in 2004. It was a network to connect Harvard University students to each other in the United States. It then quickly spread to other universities around the country. In 2006, what became

Mark Zuckerberg, founder of Facebook

better known as Facebook was opened to everyone in the world of at least 13 years of age. And the rest is social media history.

Club Penguin was a popular site with kids.

Demand for Facebook grew quickly. In April 2008, two years after it became open to the public, Facebook beat MySpace in the number of unique visits worldwide. Facebook reported that by the end of 2017 it had 2.2 billion active monthly users worldwide. That means billions of people were logging in at least once a month.

Facebook may have set its age limit for registering at 13 years, but kids had other choices for connecting online. One of the most successful was Club Penguin, a virtual world launched in 2005.

Almost nothing like it had been tried before. Club Penguin was popular with its target audience for nearly 12 years. Users created and named their own penguin avatars. Then a whole world of fun opened up. The popular game ended in 2017, replaced by Club Penguin Island. But gaming had become another big way to connect and socialize on the internet.

 Cutting edge social media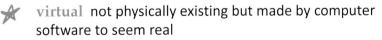

Before the term *social media* even came into use, a multimedia company called Purple Moon made computer games with a social aspect for pre-teen girls. Users shared thousands of private messages through an internal "postcard" system. They also swapped digital icons called virtual treasures. Purple Moon, launched in 1997, proved how popular social media could be. For the two years that it operated, the site had about 240,000 registered users. Mattel dominated the pre-teen gaming industry for girls with its Barbie games. It bought Purple Moon and then shut it down.

 virtual not physically existing but made by computer software to seem real

 target audience particular group that a book, film, TV series or product is aimed at

avatar computer icon used to represent a person

Do you want a fantasy world where you role-play with thousands of others around the world? And do you want to chat with them at the same time? That's what online role-playing games offer computer users. These games are another popular way people connect and socialize on the internet.

Sites that allow users in various locations to play games together have a long history. The first multi-user dungeon game came along in 1978 in the United States. By 1979 it had an international base of players. In 1987 a multiplayer adventure game called Habitat launched. Then, in the late 1990s, came massive multiplayer role-playing games (MMORPGs). MMORPGs had realistic, three-dimensional colour graphics and great sound effects that users couldn't resist. Many of the virtual worlds became massive hits in the real world.

Online games allow users to live in a fantasy world where they can be heroes.

Everquest was one of the first and biggest. Released by Sony Online Entertainment in 1999, it led the pack until 2004. Then other MMORPGs overtook Everquest. Every game developer was looking for ways to outdo its competitors. By the turn of the 21st century, gaming was a very profitable business. And it still is.

CHAPTER 4

SHARING – A MIXED BAG

Gaming is only one of the many ways to connect online. Social media is another, often with big benefits. It's one of the best and fastest ways to raise money for important causes and favourite projects. Social media also helps people to easily keep up to date with who's doing what. People use social media to find old friends or make new ones. People also use social media to keep up with one another, and with the news.

Social media connects people around the world who would otherwise never meet.

But sometimes sharing can lead a person down the wrong path. Here's one way that can happen: you come across a piece of information you agree with, disagree with or just feel strongly about. What do you do? You share it. And so does everybody else.

Understanding the difference between real and fake news is the first step in media literacy.

But often the stuff being shared is not true. It is fake but posing as real, fact-based information. Most people don't stop to research the facts on such posts. They just pass them on. This is how false information spreads so far and wide and ends up being thought of as the truth. Everyone believes it, even if it's completely made up. And that's bad.

Here's the bottom line: always think twice about what and with whom you share information. Sites such as Facebook may be the place to go for news about family and friends. But they're also loaded with false information in many forms. Facebook has been host to thousands of fake political ads and news stories.

DID YOU KNOW?

From 2015 to 2017 a Russian organization called Internet Research Agency placed at least 3,000 fake ads on Facebook, most of them political. About 10 million people saw the ads. The most popular fake US political stories on Facebook in 2016 got 10.6 million shares and comments.

FAKE NEWS IS A REAL PROBLEM

Total Facebook engagement for top 20 US election stories
(August – Election Day, 8 November 2016)

Fake news	8.7 million
Mainstream news	7.3 million

Source: Buzzsumo via Buzzfeed

This fake news is intended to sway public opinion, for example about candidates in political elections. Facebook's founder, Mark Zuckerberg, is working with the US government to stop the meddling. They're looking for ways to reduce the problem and protect users.

But meanwhile, before you share anything, examine it closely and critically. Make sure it's accurate information. Do your own research or look for information or other sites that have a fact-checking service. Don't just believe everything you read.

Learn to tell the difference between fake news and real news. And remember that opinion and fact are two different things. A news story isn't fake just because you don't like what it says. Politicians sometimes label facts they disagree with as fake news. The information may not be fake. It may just be that they don't like it.

Clickbait crazy

You may have heard the term *clickbait* recently – because the internet is loaded with it. Clickbait is a link that makes you so curious you can't help clicking through to the linked content. Maybe the bait was an outrageous headline or a fantastic bargain. The clickbait might lead you to a site that tries to sell you something. Or to a site that makes money on every view. Here's a word to the wise: don't take the bait!

⭐ **accurate** agreeing exactly with truth or a standard

CHAPTER 5

RULES OF THE INTERNET ROAD

Social media has given young people a much wider and more global viewpoint. Sharing and declaring one's news to an ever-increasing list of friends is hard to resist. But if you're not careful it's easy to get caught in an online trap.

In other words, some social media conduct today could have unpleasant consequences later. Make sure you follow a few worthwhile rules to prevent making a wrong move when you're interacting with others online.

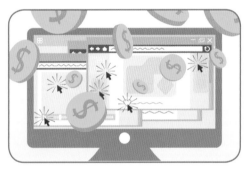

People can use your private information to make money, so be careful what you post.

DID YOU KNOW?

A lot of kids think it's safe to share things **anonymously** on apps such as Snapchat. The idea is that the messages only appear for a short time so you're safe. Think again. Cyberthieves and bullies can easily take screenshots and photos of posts and photos in the short time they're available to view.

Everybody wants to feel connected to their friends. Social media makes that easy. But when you post every detail about yourself and your life, remember that unwanted eyes may also be watching. It is very important to check your online privacy settings. Ask an adult to help. Many social media sites make all their users' information public by default. Anyone with an internet connection can see it. That means you have to change this yourself if you don't want everyone to see all your information. Many sites make it easy. They help you keep unwanted internet users from seeing your pictures, posts or personal information.

👉 Why set limits? 👈

Many popular social media sites have a minimum age – usually 13 – at which users can join. But sometimes it's as high as 17 or older. Companies set age limits to keep kids away from thieves or **predators** who want to harm them. Even if you create a secret, fake account, people you don't know may still get and use your real data. Often it's just advertisers who want to sell you things. But not always.

★ **anonymously** written, done or given by a person whose name is not known or made public

★ **default** selection made by a computer program if the user doesn't specify a choice

★ **predator** person who goes after someone or something in order to take advantage in a negative way

It is usually up to the user to set levels of privacy.

Who's watching you?

It may be surprising to know that some schools monitor their pupils' Facebook and Instagram posts (and more). They even do it when the pupils aren't at school. In the United States, for example, Florida is one state that allows this type of **surveillance**. Officials say they are checking for threatening or criminal behaviour. Do you think it is an invasion of privacy or a way to keep pupils safe? Could it be both?

On Snapchat, for example, users have multiple security choices when it comes to who can view your story or send you Snaps. On Instagram, the default is that anyone can view whatever you post. So you must choose the "Private Account" setting. Otherwise, your pictures could end up in anyone's internet search.

It might not seem like a big deal in many cases. But let's say you post a picture of yourself laughing at a crying baby. And then you try to get a babysitting job. Chances are someone who might employ you has seen the pictures. Or maybe you're applying for a place at a college or university. It's very likely that the decision-makers will look for you on social media.

There's a big difference between a real friend reaching out and a complete stranger wanting to find out more about you. So as well as privacy settings, common sense

The US military ran an advertising campaign called "Think Before You Post" to help protect its social media users.

applies. When interacting online, never send pictures or reveal your address, phone number or other personal information to someone you don't know well or at all. Even when you do know them, send the information privately rather than via a social media site.

DID YOU KNOW?

Direct messaging is popular with cyberthieves who place links that can lead to harmful downloads. Never click on a message from someone you don't know.

 surveillance act of keeping a very close watch on someone

Do you know what cyberbullying is? Have you ever done it? Lots of kids have. Cyberbullying is bullying. But it is carried out over digital devices – computers, tablets and mobile phones. It happens on social media sites, in chat rooms, through texts and emails, and on apps.

Cyberbullying may seem harmless but it often leads to depression.

It consists of mean and hurtful words or pictures. Its purpose is to shame, embarrass or show a person in a negative way.

Cyberbullying has become a huge problem. Because the internet is always on, there's little relief for the targeted kids. If you are being bullied, go offline and talk to a trusted adult about what's being said about you.

DID YOU KNOW?

In the UK, 17.9 per cent of children aged 11-15 have been victims of cyberbullying. Girls are twice as likely to report cyberbullying as boys.

Even if you've never experienced cyberbullying yourself, imagine what it must be like. No one deserves to suffer from bullying behaviour.

Social media is a wonderful tool when used properly. You can learn more about friends, and the world, and see cute pictures of pets. It's not so wonderful when it's used to spread false information or to hurt someone else. So – enjoy social media! Put your media literacy to work as an informed digital citizen.

You can help prevent cyberbullying! Don't do it and don't let your friends bully other kids.

 **Try this!**

You have the choice to make a valuable difference in the world. Many young people have gained public attention for tweeting positive comments rather than negative ones. They use online video channels and other social media to do good things. They showcase talented friends, raise money for medical research or organize food banks for the poor. There's no end to the good a person can do online.

GLOSSARY

accurate agreeing exactly with truth or a standard

analyse examine something carefully in order to understand it

anonymously written, done or given by a person whose name is not known or made public

avatar computer icon used to represent a person

cyberspace online world of computer networks

default selection made by a computer program if the user doesn't specify a choice

modem piece of electronic equipment that sends information between computers by telephone lines

predator person who goes after someone or something in order to take advantage in a negative way

predigital before the time of computer technology

reunite bring together again

social media websites and software applications that allow users to connect through the internet

surveillance act of keeping a very close watch on someone

target audience particular group that a book, film, TV series or product is aimed at

virtual not physically existing but made by computer software to seem real

FIND OUT MORE

BOOKS

Computer Programming: Learn It, Try It (Science Brain Builders), Brad Edelman (Raintree, 2018)

Cyberbullying (Tech Safety Tips), Heather E Schwartz (Raintree, 2017)

Let's Think About the Internet and Social Media, Alex Woolf (Raintree, 2014)

Mark Zuckerberg (Titans of Business), Dennis Fertig (Raintree, 2013)

WEBSITES

www.bbc.co.uk/newsround/44074704
Learn more about how to stay safe online.

www.dkfindout.com/uk/computer-coding/what-is-internet
Find out more about the internet.

COMPREHENSION QUESTIONS

1. What were two of the earliest developments in computer technology? What were the advantages of each?
2. How has digital technology changed the world for the better? What are some ways that it has made things worse? Do you think it's a benefit to be able to be "wired" all the time? Why or why not?
3. What might cause a person to participate in cyberbullying? How can this bullying activity be prevented?

INDEX